Take a closer look
at your eyes /

TAKE A CLOSER LOOK AT YOUR

Eyes

BY JANET SLIKE

Published by The Child's World®
1980 Lookout Drive • Mankato, MN 56003-1705
800-599-READ • www.childsworld.com

Acknowledgments
The Child's World®: Mary Berendes, Publishing Director
Red Line Editorial: Editorial direction and production
The Design Lab: Design
Content Consultant: Jeffrey W. Oseid, MD

Photographs ©: iStockphoto, title, 23; Artville, title;
Shutterstock Images, title, 5, 8; Alila Sao Mai/Shutterstock
Images, 6; Design Pics/Thinkstock, 9; Zoonar/Thinkstock,
11; Hemera/Thinkstock, 13; Comstock/Thinkstock, 14;
iStockphoto/Thinkstock, 16, 24; Goodshoot/Thinkstock, 19;
Valuline/Thinkstock, 21

Front cover: iStockphoto; Artville; Shutterstock Images

ISBN: 978-1623235444
LCCN: 2013931396

Printed in the United States of America
Mankato, MN
July, 2013
PA02175

About the Author

Janet Slike is a freelance editor and writer. Her short stories for adults have appeared in the anthology *Columbus: Past, Present, Future* and several magazines.

Table of Contents

CHAPTER 1

What Are Eyes?

You and your friends are having a snowball fight. You see it coming. A snowball speeds your way, but it doesn't hit bare skin. That's a relief! In the winter, you dress in layers to stay warm and dry. Your amazing eyes also have many layers to protect them.

You learn a lot about the world through your eyes. To do such a big job, the eyes have two million parts. Let's learn about some of them.

Your eyes are busy helping you see and learn.

Over each eye is a top and bottom lid. These lids are called eyelids. The eyelid is a layer of thin skin that protects the eyes and helps them stay clean. Eyelids are like your winter coat, since both are outside layers. When you see bright lights, you shut your eyes without thinking. The eyelids keep fluid in your eyes when you sleep. Eyeballs are naturally wet and feel like peeled grapes. You do not want them to feel like dry raisins!

Stuck to the eyelids are hairs called eyelashes. They keep out dust and small **particles**. Dust in the eyes makes them itchy. Eyelids and eyelashes are not a part of the actual eyes.

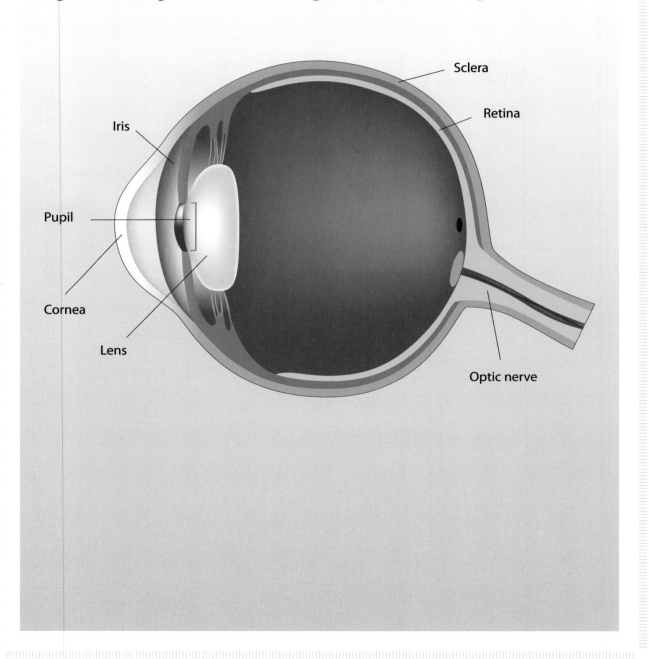

The eyeballs are marble shaped. They are an inch around when you are a teenager. The eyeballs will not grow any bigger than this. The eyes belong to the nervous system. They sit in holes called sockets, which are a part of the skull. There is a socket on each side of your nose.

The next layer is like a heavy sweater. The **cornea** covers the front of the eye. It is an odd organ because it does not have blood vessels. It receives nutrients through the **aqueous humor**, a liquid.

The white part of the eye is the **sclera**. It is a tough outer coat made of tissue. The sclera helps control eye movements.

The **iris** is in the middle of the eye. It controls how much light enters the eye. When you say what eye color you have, you are talking about your iris. People with blue eyes have less pigment, or color, in their irises than people with brown eyes. Eye color is a **genetic** trait. Your parents gave you genes for a certain eye color.

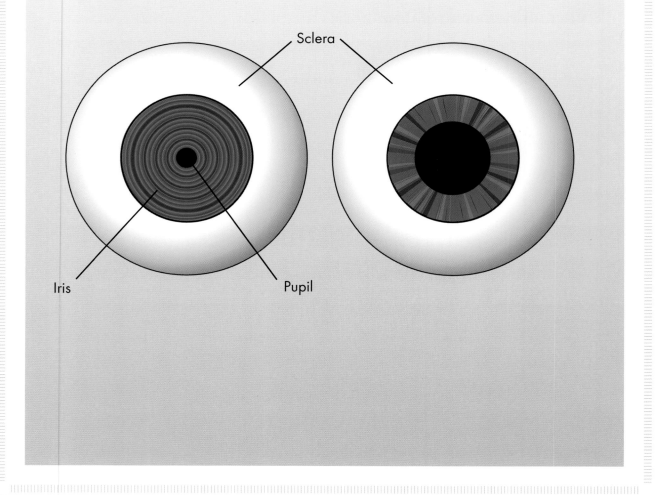

Sclera

Iris

Pupil

The **pupil** is the black circle in the center of the iris. Light goes through the pupil on its way to the **retina**. The pupil changes size depending on the amount of light. Your pupil gets bigger to let in light when you are in a dark room. Your pupil gets smaller to block extra light when you are in the sunshine. Behind the pupil lies the **lens**. Its thousands of small fibers send light to the retina.

The eyelids shut tight when there is bright sunshine.

You can choose paint for an art project because of your retina. It has special cells called **cones** that let us see colors. The cells are shaped like ice cream cones. **Rods** are rectangular cells that help us see motion. They also help us see at night. There is a big optic nerve at the back of the eye. It sends images to your brain.

Long ago, pirates believed wearing earrings would improve their eyesight. They thought the metal in earrings had magical powers.

Special cells shaped like ice cream cones help us see colors.

CHAPTER 2

What Do the Eyes Do?

What happens when you see your dog? Before you pet him, you need to know he is there. Light bounces off your dog and reaches your eye. The cornea and lens bend the light. Then an image is sent to the retina.

The image is not quite right. It is upside down. The optic nerve sends the image to your brain. Your brain makes the image right side up. Babies cannot do this right away. Their world is upside down for a few days.

Not all animals have two eyes. The sea scallop has up to 100 eyes!

The image is also reversed. Your dog is holding up his right paw to shake. But the image shows him raising his left paw. Your brain fixes that, too.

Your brain helps your eyes see your dog the right way.

CHAPTER 3

Why Do You Need Eyes?

Sight is not possible without the eyes. People do live without sight. A baby could be born blind. A person can become blind from an accident or an illness. Some people are legally blind. This means they may have some sight.

Some visually impaired people know Braille.

Visually impaired people adapt. They read and write using a special language called Braille. Raised dots replace printed letters in Braille. The reader uses touch to read the words on a page. About one in ten blind people know the Braille language.

A visually impaired person might need a cane or Seeing Eye dog when walking. Blind and visually impaired people can lead productive lives despite their disability. Famous blind people include Olympic skier Brian McKeever, singer Stevie Wonder, and marathon runner Marla Runyan.

Louis Braille created the Braille system when he was just 15 years old!

CHAPTER 4

Problems with the Eyes

Regular eye checkups are important. Maybe you visit the eye doctor before a new school year. The eye doctor checks your eyes to see if you need glasses. People wear glasses for different eye problems.

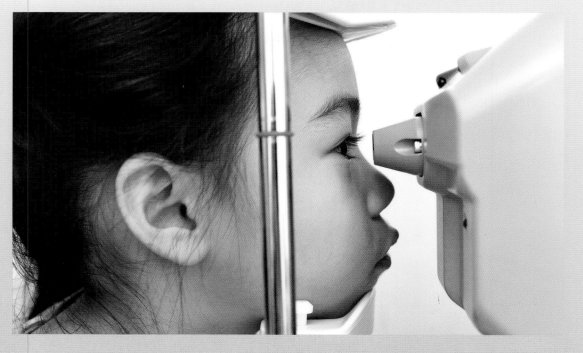

Visiting the eye doctor is important for healthy eyes.

People who can see things up close are nearsighted. They cannot see things far away very well. People who are farsighted can see things far away. They have a hard time seeing close things. Glasses or contacts will help a person see better.

People with defective cones cannot see colors properly. This means they are colorblind. More males are colorblind than females. Most colorblind people can tell when things are different colors. They just confuse a few colors. The most commonly confused colors are red and green.

As people age, they may notice their vision is cloudy. The eye lens may have spots called cataracts. Doctors can remove the spots or put in a new lens.

When there is too much pressure in the eye, a person may have **glaucoma**. This eye disease is caused when the iris presses against the pupil. The aqueous humor is trapped, making it hard to see.

CHAPTER 5

Keeping Your Eyes Healthy

Have you heard that eating carrots improves eyesight? Carrots are a great source of vitamin A. So are other vegetables. Your eyes need vitamins A, C, and E in normal amounts. But eating extra vegetables won't make your vision perfect.

Don't tell your teacher your homework is not finished because reading hurts your eyes. Your eyes might be tired, but you can still read. Have fun reading books or working on the computer. It is also good to rest your eyes. If your eyes feel dry, blink a lot. Then your eyes won't feel like raisins!

The average person blinks 12 times a minute. That is about 10,000 blinks in an average day!

It is true that good quality sunglasses protect your eyes on sunny days. You can make a health statement and a fashion statement at the same time.

Eating vegetables helps keep your eyes healthy.

Most eye injuries happen to people younger than 25 years old. Follow these tips to avoid eye problems:

- Do not put anything in your eyes. If something gets in your eye, do not rub your eye or try to remove the object. Let an adult know.
- Chemistry experiments with foaming, color-changing liquids are fun, but they can be dangerous. Always wear goggles when doing chemistry experiments, and make sure an adult is watching.
- Injuries can happen during sports games and practices. Wear eye gear during contact sports.

You may not have Superman's x-ray vision, but your eyes are super! Take good care of them.

It's important to keep your eyes safe while playing with friends.

aqueous humor (AK-we-uhs HYOO-mur) The aqueous humor is the fluid between the cornea and the lens. The cornea receives nutrients from the aqueous humor.

cones (KOHNS) Cones are the triangular cells in the retina. Cones let the eyes see color.

cornea (KOR-nee-uh) The cornea is a coating over the iris and pupil. The cornea covers the front of the eyeball and lets light through.

genetic (juh-NET-ik) Traits that are inherited from parents' traits are genetic. Eye color is a genetic trait.

glaucoma (GLAW-koh-muh) Glaucoma is a disease caused by too much eye pressure. Glaucoma happens when the iris pushes on the pupil.

iris (EYE-riss) The iris is the circular, colored portion of the eye. The iris controls how much light enters the eye.

lens (LENZ) The lens is the part of the eye that focuses light on the retina. The lens has thousands of small fibers.

particles (PAR-tuh-kuhls) Particles are small objects that can get in the eye. When particles get in the eye, it will hurt.

pupil (PYOO-puhl) The pupil is the opening of the iris through which light enters. The pupil changes size depending on the amount of light.

retina (RET-uhn-uh) The retina is the part of the eye that receives an image from the lens. The retina has special cells called cones.

rods (RODS) Rods are the rectangular cells in the retina. Rods help the eye see motion.

sclera (SKLEER-uh) The sclera is the white membrane around the eye. The sclera helps control eye movements.

LEARN MORE

BOOKS

Simon, Seymour. *Eyes and Ears*. New York: HarperCollins, 2003.

Stewart, Melissa. *The Eyes Have It: The Secrets of Eyes and Seeing*. New York: Marshall Cavendish, 2010.

WEB SITES

Visit our Web site for links about the eyes: **childsworld.com/links**

Note to Parents, Teachers, and Librarians: We routinely verify our Web links to make sure they are safe and active sites. So encourage your readers to check them out!

INDEX

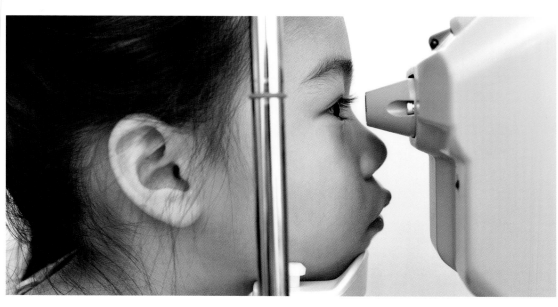